THIS CANDLEWICK BOOK BELONGS TO:

_____

_____

_____

To JJ and WR: Keep shining! ⁓ S. D.
To Sam and Ben ⁓ B. L.

Text copyright © 2003 by Susan Devins
Illustrations copyright © 2003 by Barbara Lehman

First paperback edition 2007

Library of Congress Cataloging-in-Publication Data is available.
Library of Congress Catalog Card Number 2004295148
ISBN 978-0-7636-1632-8 (hardcover)
ISBN 978-0-7636-3515-2 (paperback)

10 9 8 7 6 5 4 3 2 1

Printed in China

This book was typeset in Sassoon Primary.
The illustrations were done in watercolor and ink.

Candlewick Press
2067 Massachusetts Avenue
Cambridge, Massachusetts 02140
visit us at www.candlewick.com

The word *cookie* comes from the Dutch *koekje*,
meaning "small cake," but the first sweet cookie, full
of dates, honey, and almonds, came from the Middle East.
By the Middle Ages, sweet cookies were popular
in every part of Europe.

Christmas Cookies!

A Holiday Cookbook

Susan Devins

illustrated by Barbara Lehman

CANDLEWICK PRESS
CAMBRIDGE, MASSACHUSETTS

Contents

Christmas and cookies: what a cool combination! Can you imagine Christmas without the sweet, spicy, chocolaty aroma of home-baked cookies floating through your house?

Turning out a batch of cookies is easy and fun—measuring, mixing, rolling, icing, sneaking samples of candy decorations— and you get to eat the results of your efforts!

Cookie baking is a great time to share funny stories and baking secrets with your family and friends. You won't be able to resist making Gingerbread People, Snickerdoodles, Christmas Cracklers, Jelly Thumbprints, Rudolph's Kisses, Snowballs, White Chocolate Haystacks, and, of course, Super Sugar Cookies. You can hang your cookies from the tree as ornaments, swap them with your pals, or give them as gifts.

And don't forget to leave a plate out for Santa.

HAPPY BAKING!

Cookie Baking Basics

Read each recipe all the way through before you start.

Wash your hands.

Preheat the oven for 15 minutes before baking.

Measure dry ingredients by spooning into graduated dry measuring cups and leveling off the excess with a knife. Measure liquid ingredients in a glass measuring cup.

Always ask an adult to help you if you are using an electric mixer. Start the mixer slowly and always stop it before adding more ingredients. When creaming butter and sugar, beat until light and fluffy. Creaming may also be done with a metal or wooden spoon. Then add dry ingredients in small amounts.

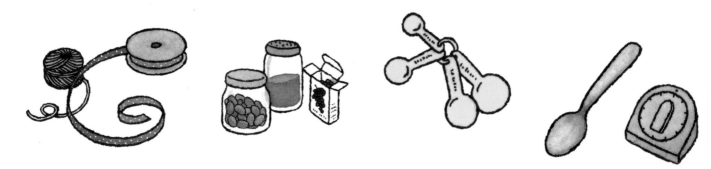

Let butter and eggs warm up to room temperature before baking. This makes mixing easier.

When rolling dough, place it between two sheets of wax paper, or roll it out on a lightly floured surface.

With rolled cookies, cut from the edge of the dough to the center, as close together as possible. Remove the cookies with a spatula to transfer them to a cookie sheet.

Always use oven mitts when removing hot cookie sheets.

Check cookies a minute before suggested baking time to make sure they don't burn.

Super Sugar Cookies

The possibilities for this all-time classic Christmas cookie
are as wide as your imagination!

1 cup (250 ml) (2 sticks) unsalted
   butter at room temperature
1 cup (250 ml) sugar
1 egg
2 teaspoons (10 ml) vanilla
2¼ cups (550 ml) all-purpose flour
1 teaspoon (5 ml) baking powder
pinch of salt

(Makes about 3 dozen)

1 In a large bowl cream butter and sugar until light and fluffy. Beat in egg and vanilla until smooth.

2 In a separate bowl combine flour, baking powder, and salt. Add gradually to the creamed mixture until it forms a soft dough. Divide the dough into two parts, cover each with plastic wrap, and refrigerate for one to three hours.

3 Preheat oven to 350°F (180°C). Lightly grease cookie sheets. Using one portion of dough at a time, roll between two pieces of wax paper or on a lightly floured surface to ⅛ inch (.3 cm) thickness.

4 Cut into desired shapes using cookie cutters. Place cookies 1 inch (2.5 cm) apart on cookie sheets. Bake for 8–10 minutes, until set and edges are lightly golden.

5 Remove cookie sheets from oven and cool for two minutes. Transfer cookies to a wire rack to cool completely.

6 When cool, decorate with frosting, colored sugars, nuts, or candies. Tips and recipes are on pages 34–35.

Ornaments: To hang the cookies as ornaments, use a chopstick, straw, or toothpick to punch out a hole near the top of each unbaked cookie. Loop licorice, ribbon, or colored yarn through the holes after cookies are baked.

Gift Tags: To make Super Sugar Cookies into gift tags, cut dough into 2 inch x 4 inch (5 cm x 10 cm) rectangles and bake as directed. When cooled, write the names of your gift recipients with one of the icings on page 35. Wrap each gift tag in cellophane and attach it to your gift with a colorful ribbon. What a great personal touch for your Christmas present!

Santa Claus Cookies

Make your own version of a jolly Santa!

To decorate cookies:

3 tablespoons (45 ml) red sugar
½ cup (125 ml) shredded coconut
30 mini marshmallows
60 raisins
30 cinnamon red hot candies

(Makes 30)

1 Use **Super Sugar Cookies** recipe (page 8) and cut the dough into circles.

2 Spread **Basic Buttercream Frosting** (page 34) or **Icing Paint** (page 35) on base of cookie.

3 Sprinkle red sugar on top third of cookie for hat. Sprinkle shredded coconut on bottom third for Santa's beard. Press one marshmallow on top for tassel of hat, two raisins for eyes, and one cinnamon red hot for nose.

The legend of Santa Claus rose out of the story of St. Nicholas, a fourth century bishop from Myra, in what is now Turkey. The charitable man was very kind to children, and often gave anonymous gifts. The red and white of our modern Santa's suit stems from the color of his bishop's hat and cape.

Red & Green Polka-Dot Cookies

Leave these out for Santa and watch them disappear!

1 cup (250 ml) (2 sticks) unsalted
   butter at room temperature
1 cup (250 ml) brown sugar
¾ cup (175 ml) sugar
2 eggs
1 teaspoon (5 ml) vanilla
2 cups (500 ml) all-purpose flour
1 teaspoon (5 ml) baking soda
1 teaspoon (5 ml) salt
1½ cups (375 ml) red and green
   M&M's

(Makes about 6 dozen)

1 Preheat oven to 375°F (190°C). Grease cookie sheets.

2 In a large bowl cream butter, brown sugar, and sugar until light and fluffy. Add the eggs and vanilla and mix well.

3 In a separate bowl sift together the flour, baking soda, and salt. Add gradually to the creamed mixture until blended. Stir in M&M's.

4 Place by teaspoonfuls (5 ml) 1 inch (2.5 cm) apart on cookie sheets and bake for 8–10 minutes, until brown around the edges. Remove from oven and leave cookies on sheet for five minutes. Remove to a wire rack to cool completely.

Candy Cane Cookies

It wouldn't be Christmas without candy canes,
so why not try this nifty baked version!

½ cup (125 ml) (1 stick) unsalted
   butter at room temperature
½ cup (125 ml) vegetable
   shortening
1 cup (250 ml) powdered sugar
1 egg
1½ teaspoons (7 ml) peppermint
   extract
1½ teaspoons (7 ml) vanilla
2½ cups (625 ml) all-purpose flour
1 teaspoon (5 ml) salt
½ teaspoon (2 ml) red food
   coloring
½ cup (125 ml) sugar

(Makes about 4 dozen)

1 In a large bowl cream butter and shortening. Add powdered sugar and mix well. Beat in egg, peppermint extract, and vanilla. Blend in flour and salt.

2 Divide the dough in half. Tint one half with red food coloring. Cover each portion of dough and refrigerate for one hour.

3 Preheat oven to 375°F (190°C). Take 1 teaspoonful (5 ml) of dough of each color and form each into a 5-inch (13 cm) rope. Place ropes side by side. Then press together and twist, curving the top into a candy-cane shape.

4 Place about 2 inches (5 cm) apart on ungreased cooking sheets. Bake for 11–12 minutes, until very light brown. Sprinkle with sugar while still warm. Cool on wire racks.

The hooked shape of the candy cane represents the
crook of the shepherds who were present at the Nativity.
Bobs Candies in Albany, Georgia, the company that invented
the automated candy cane manufacturing machine in the 1950s,
is the largest producer of candy canes in the world today.

Gingerbread People

"Run, run as fast as you can.
You can't catch me, I'm the gingerbread man."

¾ cup (175 ml) (1½ sticks)
   unsalted butter at room
   temperature
¾ cup (175 ml) dark brown sugar
½ cup (125 ml) unsulphured
   molasses
1 egg
3 cups (750 ml) all-purpose flour
1 teaspoon (5 ml) baking soda
¼ teaspoon (1 ml) salt
1½ teaspoons (7 ml) ground ginger
1 teaspoon (5 ml) cinnamon
½ teaspoon (2 ml) nutmeg
¼ teaspoon (1 ml) ground cloves

(Makes about 40)

1 In a large bowl cream butter and brown sugar until light and fluffy. Add molasses and egg and beat until blended.

2 In a separate bowl sift together flour, baking soda, salt, ground ginger, cinnamon, nutmeg, and ground cloves and then whisk together to combine evenly. Gradually add to the creamed mixture and blend well.

3 Divide the dough in half and wrap each piece in plastic. Refrigerate for two hours or until dough is firm enough to roll out.

4 Preheat oven to 350°F (180°C). Take out one piece of dough and roll out to about ⅛ inch (.3 cm) thickness between sheets of wax paper or on a lightly floured board. Cut out gingerbread people shapes and use a spatula to transfer them to ungreased cookie sheets.

5 Bake for 8–10 minutes, until light brown (don't burn). Allow the cookies to cool slightly on the sheets for one minute and then transfer to wire racks to cool completely.

6 When the cookies are still hot, press raisins or candies into the dough for eyes and buttons. Or cool the cookies and decorate with **Royal Icing** (page 35) to attach decorations.

Baking Tip: To make gingerbread hair, put raw dough through a garlic press. Attach "hair" to the gingerbread people before baking.

Christmas Wreaths

You won't get a chance to hang these on your door—
they'll be snapped up and eaten as soon as they're cool.

2 tablespoons (30 ml) unsalted
butter
24 large or 2 cups (500 ml) mini
marshmallows
1 teaspoon (5 ml) vanilla
1 teaspoon (5ml) green food
coloring
3 cups (750 ml) Rice Krispies
cinnamon red hot candies

(Makes about 6 large wreaths)

1 Line cookie sheets with wax paper.

2 In a large saucepan heat butter and marshmallows over low heat, stirring until marshmallows are melted.

3 Remove from heat and stir in vanilla and green food coloring. Stir in Rice Krispies until well covered.

4 With lightly greased hands, use about ½ cup (125 ml) mixture and, working quickly, shape into wreath forms. Place on cookie sheets.

5 Decorate with cinnamon red hot candies while wreaths are still sticky. Cool completely.

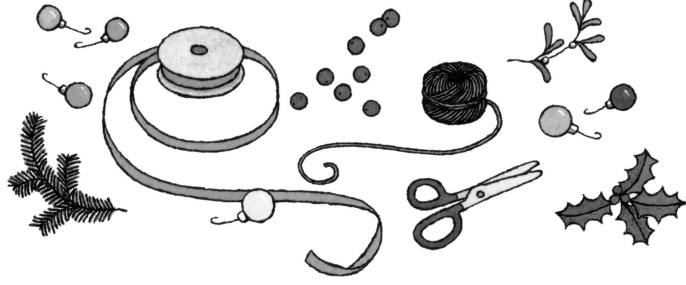

The modern Christmas custom of displaying a wreath on the front door of a home is borrowed from Ancient Rome. Romans wished each other "good health" in the new year by exchanging branches of evergreens. They called these gifts *strenae*, after Strenia, goddess of health. It became the custom to bend these branches into a ring and display them on doorways. The Christmas wreath, like the evergreens used as Christmas trees, symbolizes the strength of life overcoming the forces of winter. Also, during the Middle Ages, red holly berries were believed to keep witches out of the home. That is why holly became the traditional and lucky evergreen for wreath making.

Stained Glass Christmas Trees

The designs in these trees hold dazzling, multicolored candies that sparkle like "stained glass."

½ cup (125 ml) vegetable shortening

½ cup (125 ml) (1 stick) unsalted butter at room temperature

1 cup (250 ml) sugar

2 eggs

1 teaspoon (5 ml) vanilla

2½ cups (625 ml) all-purpose flour

1 teaspoon (5 ml) baking powder

1 teaspoon (5 ml) salt

6 packages of Life Savers (5-flavor)

(Makes about 40)

1 In a large bowl cream shortening, butter, and sugar until light and fluffy. Add eggs and vanilla.

2 Mix dry ingredients in a separate bowl and gradually blend into creamed mixture. Divide dough in half and cover each piece with plastic wrap. Chill for one hour.

3 Preheat oven to 375°F (190°C). Working with one piece at a time, roll out dough between two pieces of wax paper or on lightly floured surface to about ⅛ inch (.3 cm) thickness.

4 Using Christmas tree cookie cutters, cut into shapes. Use either smaller cookie cutters (or make your own patterns, with an adult's help) and cut out small shapes within the trees for "stained glass windows."

5 Place cookies on foil-covered cookie sheets. Place whole or crushed Life Savers in the "windows," filling until candy is level with dough. Bake for 7–9 minutes, until candy is melted. Let cool completely on cookie sheets. Remove very carefully.

Royalty was responsible for popularizing the Christmas tree throughout the United Kingdom. Prince Albert, Queen Victoria's German-born husband, had a Christmas tree set up in Windsor Castle in 1841 to remind him of his homeland traditions.
The first Christmas trees in the United States were introduced in the early 1800s by German settlers in Pennsylvania.

Chocolate Superstars

These cutouts will make you a baking superstar!

¾ cup (175 ml) (1½ sticks) unsalted butter at room temperature

1¼ cups (300 ml) sifted powdered sugar

1 large egg, lightly beaten

½ teaspoon (2 ml) vanilla

1½ cups (375 ml) all-purpose flour

⅔ cup (150 ml) unsweetened cocoa powder

¼ teaspoon (1 ml) salt

¼ teaspoon (1 ml) cinnamon

(Makes about 3 dozen)

1 In a large bowl cream butter and sugar until light and fluffy. Beat in egg and vanilla.

2 In a separate bowl sift together flour, cocoa powder, salt, and cinnamon. Add gradually to the creamed mixture until combined.

3 Place dough in plastic wrap and chill for one hour.

4 Preheat oven to 350°F (180°C). On floured surface roll dough to ⅛ inch (.3 cm). Cut out shapes with star cutters and transfer with spatula to ungreased cookie sheets. Refrigerate until firm, about 15 minutes. Bake for 8–10 minutes, until crisp. Cool on wire rack.

5 Decorate following the tips and recipes on pages 34–35.

The tradition of the modern Christmas tree has often been attributed
to Martin Luther, the father of the German Reformation. The legend goes
that returning home on a snowy Christmas Eve in 1517, he was struck by the
beauty of the sparkling stars above. In order to re-create this spectacle for his
family, he dug up a small fir tree and put it in the nursery. He then
lit up its branches with candles, just as the starlit trees
outside had appeared to him.

Rudolph's Kisses

What a treat when you bite into the surprise filling!

1 cup (250 ml) (2 sticks) unsalted
    butter at room temperature
½ cup (125 ml) sugar
2 teaspoons (10 ml) vanilla
2 cups (500 ml) all-purpose flour
¼ teaspoon (1 ml) salt
36–48 chocolate kisses
1 cup (250 ml) powdered sugar

(Makes about 3 dozen)

1 Preheat oven to 350°F
(180°C).

2 In a large bowl cream
butter and sugar until light
and fluffy. Add vanilla
and mix.

3 Add flour and salt to
creamed mixture and beat
until well mixed.

4 Wrap one tablespoon
(15 ml) of dough around
each chocolate kiss.
Place 1 inch (2.5 cm) apart
on ungreased cookie sheets
and bake for 18–20 minutes.
Cookies should not brown.

5 When cool, roll the
cookies in powdered sugar.

Rudolph the red-nosed reindeer was created by an advertising writer for the Montgomery Ward department store chain in Chicago in 1939. Robert May wrote the story about the reindeer with a shiny red nose for the store's Christmas giveaway coloring book. The story was printed commercially in 1947. It was turned into a musical version by songwriter Johnny Marks. In 1949 the song was recorded by Gene Autry. "Rudolph the Red-Nosed Reindeer" sold two million copies the first year.

Jelly Thumbprints

Individualize these cookies with your very own fingerprints.

1 cup (250 ml) (2 sticks) unsalted
   butter at room temperature
½ cup (125 ml) sugar
2 eggs, separated
   (ask an adult to help)
2 teaspoons (10 ml) vanilla
2 cups (500 ml) all-purpose flour
2 cups (500 ml) finely crushed
   corn flakes
jelly or jam

(Makes about 60)

1 Preheat oven to 350°F (180°C). Lightly grease cookie sheets.

2 Cream butter and sugar until light and fluffy. Beat in egg yolks and vanilla. Blend in flour.

3 Shape into small balls. Dip into unbeaten egg whites and roll in crushed corn flakes. Place 1 inch (2.5 cm) apart on cookie sheets. Make a depression in the center of each cookie, using your thumb, the end of a chopstick, or a wooden spoon handle.

4 Bake for 10–12 minutes, until just firm.
(If indentation is not strong enough when cookies come out of oven, re-press with wooden spoon handle.)

5 Cool the cookies on the sheets. Using a small spoon, fill centers with your favorite jelly or jam.

White Chocolate Haystacks

Sweet, salty, crunchy, crackly—all rolled into one winter confection.

12 ounces (375 g) white chocolate, chopped

1½ cups (375 ml) peanuts

1½ cups (375 ml) thin pretzel sticks, broken into 1-inch (2.5 cm) pieces

(Makes about 30)

1 Line cookie sheets with wax paper.

2 Melt chocolate in the top of a double boiler (or in the microwave on medium heat for two minutes), stirring until smooth. (Ask an adult for help.) Add the nuts and pretzels, stirring until coated with chocolate.

3 Remove the pan from the heat and spoon the mixture onto cookie sheets by rounded teaspoonfuls (5 ml) to look like small haystacks. Cool to room temperature.

The popular Christmas song "Jingle Bells" was composed in 1857 by James Pierpont and was originally called "One-Horse Open Sleigh."

Snickerdoodles

A cookie that's incredibly edible.

1 cup (250 ml) (2 sticks) unsalted butter at room temperature

1½ cups (375 ml) sugar

2 eggs

2 cups (500 ml) all-purpose flour

2 teaspoons (10 ml) cream of tartar

1 teaspoon (5 ml) baking soda

¼ teaspoon (1 ml) salt

Coating:

3 tablespoons (45 ml) sugar

2 teaspoons (10 ml) cinnamon

(Makes about 4 dozen)

1 In a large bowl cream butter and sugar until light and fluffy. Add eggs one at a time and mix until well blended.

2 In a separate bowl sift together flour, cream of tartar, baking soda, and salt and mix well. Gradually add the flour mixture to the creamed mixture until dough is smooth. Cover the dough and chill for one hour.

3 Preheat oven to 375ºF (190ºC). Lightly grease cookie sheets.

4 Shape dough into 1-inch (2.5 cm) balls. Combine the sugar and cinnamon and roll the balls in this mixture. Place 2 inches (5 cm) apart on cookie sheets. Bake for 10–11 minutes, until edges are golden.

5 Transfer sheets to wire racks and let stand until cookies are firm, about two minutes. Then transfer cookies with a spatula to wire racks to cool completely.

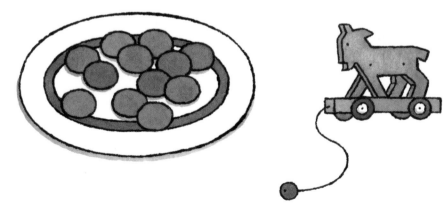

Simply Shortbread

Easy as pie—but it's shortbread!

½ cup (125 ml) cornstarch
½ cup (125 ml) powdered sugar,
    plus extra for dusting
1 cup (250 ml) all-purpose flour
1 cup (250 ml) (2 sticks) unsalted
    butter at room temperature

(Makes about 3 dozen)

1 Preheat oven to 300°F (150°C).

2 Sift cornstarch, powdered sugar, and flour together into a bowl. Blend in butter with spoon until a soft dough forms.

3 Shape into 1-inch (2.5 cm) balls. Place about 1½ inches (4 cm) apart on ungreased cookie sheets. Flatten the balls with a lightly floured fork or the bottom of a glass dipped in flour. Bake for 20–25 minutes, until edges are lightly browned.

4 Sprinkle with powdered sugar.

Christmas Cracklers

It looks like someone stepped on these cookies,
but looks are deceiving—they're a chocolate lover's dream!

1¼ cups (300 ml) all-purpose flour

½ cup (125 ml) cocoa powder

2 teaspoons (10 ml) baking powder

¼ teaspoon (1 ml) salt

½ cup (125 ml) (1 stick) unsalted
  butter at room temperature

1⅓ cups (325 ml) light brown
  sugar

2 eggs

1 teaspoon (5 ml) vanilla

8 ounces (250 g) bittersweet
  chocolate, melted and cooled
  (ask an adult to help)

⅓ cup (75 ml) milk

1 cup (250 ml) powdered sugar

(Makes about 4 dozen)

1 Preheat oven to 350°F
(180°C). Sift together flour,
cocoa powder, baking powder,
and salt in a medium bowl
and set aside.

2 In a large bowl cream
butter and brown sugar
until light and fluffy. Add
eggs and vanilla and beat
until well combined. Add
melted chocolate. Add flour
mixture, alternating each
addition with a little milk.
Mix until combined.

3 Shape pieces of dough
into 1-inch (2.5 cm) balls.
(If dough is too sticky to
handle, cover and refrigerate
for one hour.) Place the
powdered sugar on a sheet
of wax paper and roll the
balls to cover completely
with sugar. Place the balls
1 inch (2.5 cm) apart on
cookie sheets and bake for
12–14 minutes, until cookies
have flattened and look
split open.

4 Transfer cookie sheets to
wire rack to cool completely.

The first Christmas card was created in 1843 by John Calcott Horsley, an English illustrator. His card was designed like a postcard and showed a large English family enjoying the Christmas holidays. The message on the card read, "A Merry Christmas and a Happy New Year to You." By 1860 the custom of sending Christmas cards spread throughout the United Kingdom and on to other countries. The first Christmas cards produced in the United States were made in 1875 by Louis Prang, a German-born Boston printer.

Peppermint Chocolate Bark

A zesty take on chocolate bark—and full of Christmas colors.

20 ounces (600 g) mint chocolate, chopped

1 cup (250 ml) coarsely crushed red-and-white striped peppermint candy canes

1 Preheat oven to 250°F (120°C).

2 Line a 17 inch x 11 inch (43 cm x 28 cm) rimmed baking sheet with parchment paper. Sprinkle chopped mint chocolate evenly over the sheet. Place in oven until chocolate is softened, about 5 minutes. Remove from oven.

3 With a rubber spatula, spread chocolate evenly over the sheet out to the edges. Immediately sprinkle crushed peppermint candy canes over chocolate.

4 Refrigerate until chocolate is firm, about two hours. Break bark into pieces.

The first national recognition of the Christmas-tree custom in the United States came in 1856, when President Franklin Pierce decorated one at the White House. Electric Christmas lights were first used in 1895. They were introduced in the United States by Ralph E. Morris, and proved safer than traditional candles. In 1923 President Calvin Coolidge started the annual tradition of the national Christmas tree lighting ceremony on the White House lawn. America's official national Christmas tree is located in Kings Canyon National Park in California. The tree, a giant sequoia, is almost 300 feet tall.

Today some form of Christmas tree is part of nearly every Christmas celebration. Decorations include tinsel, stringed cookies, and bright ornaments. A star is mounted on top of many trees to represent the star that led the wise men to the stable in Bethlehem where Jesus was born.

Peanut Butter & Ice Cream Sandwiches

Move over, PB & J—here's PB & IC!

½ cup (125 ml) (1 stick) unsalted
   butter at room temperature

½ cup (125 ml) smooth peanut
   butter

¼ cup (50 ml) sugar

¾ cup (175 ml) firmly packed
dark brown sugar

1 egg

½ teaspoon (2 ml) vanilla

1½ cups (375 ml) all-purpose flour

½ teaspoon (2 ml) baking soda

½ teaspoon (2 ml) baking powder

¼ teaspoon (1 ml) salt

1 pint (500 ml) vanilla ice cream

(Makes about 30)

1 Preheat oven to 350°F
(180°C). Lightly grease cookie
sheets.

2 In a large bowl cream
butter and peanut butter.
Then blend in both sugars.
Add the egg and vanilla and
mix well.

3 In a separate bowl sift
together flour, baking soda,
baking powder, and salt. Beat
this mixture into the peanut
butter mixture until smooth.

4 Shape dough into balls
and place about 2 inches
(5 cm) apart on cookie sheets.
Press cookies flat with the
tines of a fork.

5 Bake for 8–10 minutes,
until lightly browned.
Remove to wire racks
to cool.

6 To make ice cream
sandwiches, place 1
rounded tablespoonful
(15 ml) of slightly softened
vanilla ice cream between
two cookies. Freeze
uncovered for one hour.
Wrap in plastic and store
in freezer.

Snowballs

These are as light and fluffy as the first winter snowfall.

1 cup (250 ml) (2 sticks) unsalted
    butter at room temperature
6 tablespoons (90 ml) sugar
1 teaspoon (5 ml) vanilla
2 cups (500 ml) all-purpose flour
1 cup (250 ml) finely chopped
    pecans
1 cup (250 ml) powdered sugar

(Makes about 4 dozen)

1 Preheat oven to 300°F (150°C).

2 In a large bowl cream butter and sugar until light and fluffy. Beat in vanilla. Gradually add flour until well blended. Stir in pecans.

3 Shape into 1-inch (2.5 cm) balls. Place about 1 inch (2.5 cm) apart on ungreased cookie sheets.

4 Bake for 30–35 minutes, until lightly golden. When still hot, roll in powdered sugar. Cool on racks and then roll again in powdered sugar.

Decorating Your Cookies

Piping Bag Use a piping bag to make dots, lines, bows, initials, noses, buttons, etc., on cookies. Fill the bag with icing. Then fit the decorating tip into the narrow end of the bag. Put the piping bag in a short cup, fold down the bag to make a cuff, and spoon the icing into the bag with a rubber spatula. Unfold the cuff, twist the top of the bag closed, and squeeze the piping bag with one hand to press out the icing.

Make your own piping bag

Fill a Ziploc plastic bag halfway with icing, squeeze out the air above, and lock it shut. Then snip off a mini-tip at the end of the bag with a pair of scissors and pipe away.

Decorating To decorate cookies after baking, use royal icing for basic coating and fine details (and as "glue" to stick on candy eyes, buttons, noses, etc.). For a pretty glaze, use icing paint or basic buttercream frosting.

Assorted Decorating Candies

Use M&M's, gumdrops, chopped nuts, raisins, colored sprinkles, colored sugars, licorice, cinnamon red hots, jelly beans, chocolate chips, sweetened shredded coconut, and button candies to decorate cookies. Place these decorations on the cookies before the icing dries.

Basic Buttercream Frosting

3 cups (750 ml) sifted powdered sugar

⅓ cup (75 ml) unsalted butter at room temperature

3 tablespoons (45 ml) hot milk

1½ teaspoons (7 ml) vanilla

Using an electric mixer, beat the powdered sugar, butter, hot milk, and vanilla on medium speed until smooth and creamy. If frosting seems too stiff, mix in one more tablespoon (15 ml) of hot milk. If it seems too runny, mix in one more tablespoon (15 ml) of powdered sugar.

Royal Icing

3 large egg whites
4 cups (1000 ml) powdered sugar

In a large mixing bowl, beat the egg whites and powdered sugar at low speed to moisten the sugar and then at high speed until very glossy and stiff peaks form (5–7 minutes). Icing can be used white, or divided into small cups and colored with food coloring. Put the icing in a piping bag and decorate.

Icing Paint

2 cups (500 ml) sifted powdered sugar
¼ cup (50 ml) water
food coloring

Combine powdered sugar with water. Brush a thin coat of icing over cookies. Allow to dry for 10 minutes. Divide remaining icing into containers and color each with food coloring.
Thin with a little water, and then paint each cookie with a paintbrush.

Happy Holidays Cookie Exchange

Here's a fun way to get your friends together this holiday season. Have a Happy Holidays Cookie Exchange and show off the dazzling array of cookies you baked!

*C*hoose a date and time with your parents or an adult who will be hosting the event with you

*I*nvite five or six friends and have each guest (including yourself) bake two dozen of one kind of their favorite cookies. Coordinate the recipes so that each person is baking a different kind of cookie. Have each friend make copies of their recipes to hand out at the party.

*O*n the day of the party make some cocoa or punch. Decorate your dining room table with a festive tablecloth, and put out pretty platters on which your guests can place their baked goods. Make a special centerpiece to highlight the occasion.

Give your guests a gift bag or paper plate and have them go around the table and select four or five cookies from each platter. (Divide the remaining cookies among the guests.) Each guest will leave with a selection of yummy cookies—all home baked!

Cool Centerpiece: To make a centerpiece in the shape of a wreath with a gingerbread cookie for each guest, begin by laying the cookies flat in a circular shape. Then decorate the gingerbread with the initial of each guest. Place a big red bow at the bottom of the centerpiece.

Gift Giving: Ask each guest to bake an extra dozen of their favorite cookies. After the party, ask an adult to take you to a homeless shelter or your favorite charity and hand-deliver these festive baked goods to the needy. Now, that's the true spirit of Christmas!

Christmas Cookies as Gifts

*T*here's no better present than homemade Christmas cookies at holiday time. Use tins, empty coffee cans, candy boxes, shoe boxes, hat boxes, egg cartons, or glass jars with wide mouths as gift containers. Wash and dry glass jars and coffee cans. Shake out all boxes and cartons. Line boxes with colored tissue paper. Line tins and coffee cans with foil. Paint the outside of boxes and cover them with stickers, or paste pretty wrapping paper on them.

Fill a clear glass jar with homemade cookies and tie a beautiful ribbon on top. Separate each layer of cookies with wax paper. Wrap individual cookies in cellophane with bows, or put a few cookies together and put them in cellophane gift bags that are available at party supply stores. String together a few cookies with ribbon or licorice. Attach your favorite cookie cutter to each gift.

Susan Devins is the author of three children's books about cooking and baking, and has also written children's entertainment columns for newspapers and magazines. Before becoming a children's book author, she worked as managing editor at *National Lampoon* magazine and as a *Variety* correspondent covering film and television. Susan Devins lives in Toronto with her husband and son.

Barbara Lehman recently won a Caldecott Honor for her book *The Red Book*. She says that in her illustrations for *Christmas Cookies!* she tried to capture "both my own early experiences with Christmas (we really did decorate our tree with nuts on strings and little houses) and the old-fashioned toy-type decorations that my elderly neighbors hung on their small tree." Barbara Lehman lives in Claverack, New York.